Mini Mike

in the New Testament

by Carl Anker Mortensen

Illustrated by José Pérez Montero

SCANDINAVIA PUBLISHING HOUSE

Mini Mike
in the New Testament

Copyright © 1996
  Scandinavia Publishing House
  Drejervej 15, 3
  DK- 2400 Copenhagen NV
  Denmark

E-mail: jvo@scanpublishing.dk
Phone +45 35 31 03 30

Text: Carl Anker Mortensen

English: Anne de Graaf

Illustrations: José Pérez Montero

Graphic design: Nils V. Glistrup

Printed in Singapore

ISBN 87 7247 440 8

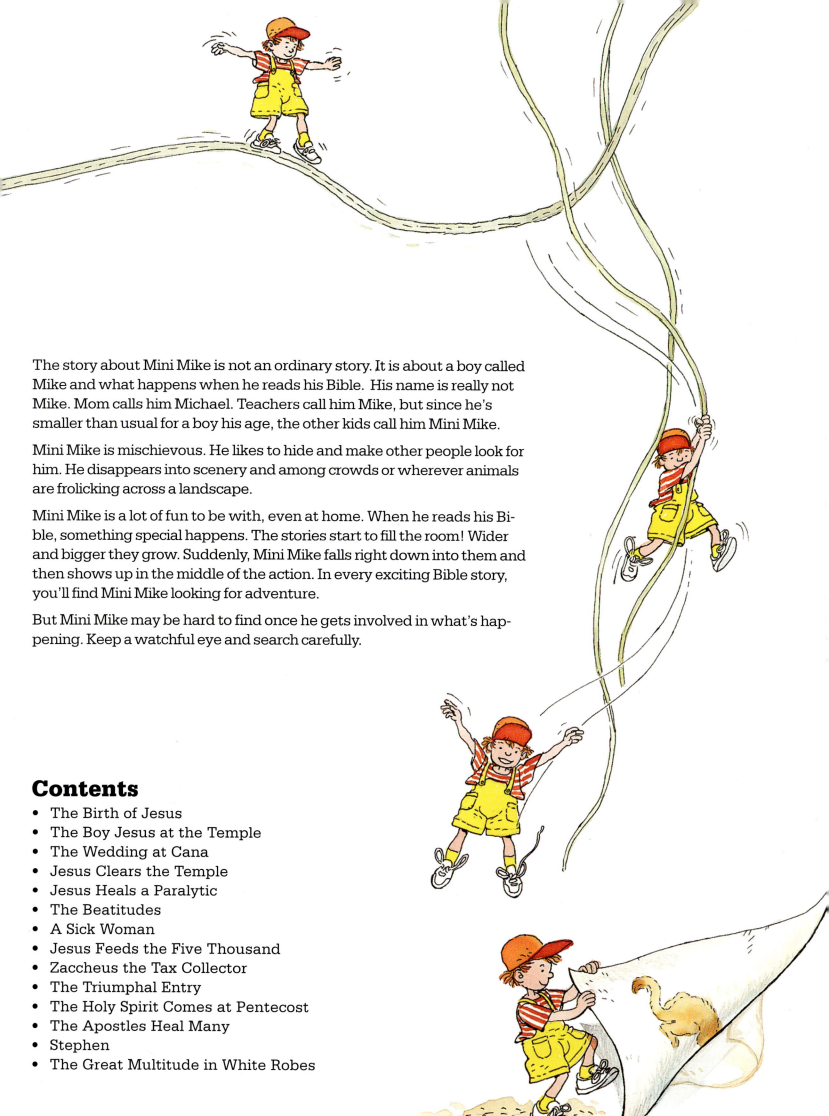

The story about Mini Mike is not an ordinary story. It is about a boy called Mike and what happens when he reads his Bible. His name is really not Mike. Mom calls him Michael. Teachers call him Mike, but since he's smaller than usual for a boy his age, the other kids call him Mini Mike.

Mini Mike is mischievous. He likes to hide and make other people look for him. He disappears into scenery and among crowds or wherever animals are frolicking across a landscape.

Mini Mike is a lot of fun to be with, even at home. When he reads his Bible, something special happens. The stories start to fill the room! Wider and bigger they grow. Suddenly, Mini Mike falls right down into them and then shows up in the middle of the action. In every exciting Bible story, you'll find Mini Mike looking for adventure.

But Mini Mike may be hard to find once he gets involved in what's happening. Keep a watchful eye and search carefully.

Contents

The Birth of Jesus

All the people you see here come from this city - Bethlehem, except for Mini Mike - he comes from (Denmark). Everybody is in Bethlehem to be counted and registered. Mike is here to see little Jesus. Can you find him? Mike is very excited. He is almost afraid to go any closer. Jesus is God's own Son. Mike knows that, but do you think the others know it? Where are the shepherds and their sheep?

Questions

1. Find the place where people go to be registered and counted.
2. No one has counted the sheep. How many are there?
3. Who do you think the three people riding on the camels are?
4. Where is the soldier about to lose his spear?
5. Can you see three children going very fast?

Read

Luke 2:1-18

Today in the town of David a Savior has been born to you; He is Christ the Lord. This will be a sign to you: You will find a baby wrapped in strips of cloth and lying in a manger.

- Luke 2:11-12

The Boy Jesus at the Temple

Here we are in Jerusalem. Jesus is now twelve years old. Sometimes, like today, He is very hard to find. Joseph and Mary have finally found Jesus in the temple. Mini Mike already knew Jesus was here, so he found Him first. It is very difficult to understand what Jesus and these old, wise men are talking about. Can you find Him? Where do you think Mini Mike is?

Questions

1. How many vendors, or people selling things, can you find?

2. Do you see the boy with a fishing pole?

3. Where is the man telling the people to be quiet.

4. What is the man on the ladder doing?

5. Can you find the butterfly?

Read

Luke 2:41-49

After three days they found Him in the temple courts, sitting among the teachers, listening to them and asking them questions. Everyone who heard Him was amazed at His understanding and His answers.

- Luke 2:46-47

The Wedding at Cana

This is quite a wedding Mike is at. No wonder they ran out of wine! And there is Jesus. He has asked the servants to pour water into the big, stone water jars. Then He has turned the water into wine. Only a couple of people know what has happened. Mike is waiting to see the surprised looks on their faces. He loves parties. He doesn't drink wine, but he would really like a coke.

Questions

1. Whose bottle has just ran out of wine?
2. Where are the two boys feeding a dog?
3. Who is on roller skates?
4. Are the bride and groom in the picture?
5. Find the servants who are about to drop something.
6. Have you seen a child riding a dog?

Read

John 2:1-11

Nearby stood six stone water jars, the kind used by the Jews for ceremonial washing, each holding from twenty to thirty gallons. Jesus said to the servants, "Fill the jars with water"; so they filled them to the brim. Then He told them, "Now draw some out and take it to the master of the banquet." They did so, and the master of the banquet tasted the water that had been turned into wine.

- John 2:6-9

Jesus Clears the Temple

Here Mike really finds out just how brave Jesus is. "Get out of here!" He cried at the people who had turned the temple courts into a market. When Jesus started turning over the tables they could see He was serious. The temple is God's house, built for prayer. It is easy to understand why the disciples look so frightened. But they know very well that Jesus only does what God wants Him to do.

Questions

1. Where is the frightened cow trying to climb a wall?
2. Find the alarm clock.
3. Where are the doves coming from?
4. Can you see a violin?
5. Do you see a calculator?
6. How many things and animals are listed in John 2:15-16? See below.

Read

John 2:12-21

So He made a whip out of cords, and drove all from the temple area, both sheep and cattle. He scattered the coins of the money changers and overturned their tables. To those who sold doves He said, "Get these out of here! How dare you turn My Father's house into a market!"

- John 2:15-16

Jesus Heals a Paralytic

"Just great!" Mike is mumbling to himself. He has given up trying to get any closer to Jesus. But the four men have not given up. They want their paralyzed friend to meet Jesus so that He can heal him. That is why they lowered down their friend on his mat. Some people think they have gone too far. Not Jesus. He wants to heal the man.

Questions

1. Do you see a mother holding a rattle for her baby?
2. Which musical instruments can you find?
3. Where is the woman who has lost her yarn?
4. Can you find a boy on a unicycle?
5. Find the man who is balancing on a chair.

Read

Mark 2:1-12

But that you may know that the Son of Man has authority on earth to forgive sins…"

He said to the paralytic, "I tell you, get up, take your mat and go home."

- Mark 2:10-12

The Beatitudes

Now, here there is room enough for everybody, and everybody is listening. Well, almost everybody. A few of the children are not paying attention to Jesus. You can hear Him from far away. "Pray", Jesus says, "then you shall be given what you are asking for." Mike thinks to himself, "I've got to remember that."

Questions

1. Can you see any animals here that you have not seen earlier in the book?
2. How many different kinds of birds are there?
3. Can you find a man walking on stilts?
4. Find the tree with the most people in it.
5. Which child cannot hear anything of what Jesus is saying?
6. Who is the farthest away from Jesus?

Read

Matthew 4:25-5:12

Now when He saw the crowds, He went up on a mountainside and sat down. His disciples came to Him, and He began to teach them, saying:

"Blessed are the poor in spirit, for theirs is the kingdom of heaven".

- Matthew. 5:1-3

A Sick Woman

Jesus is asking, "Who touched me?" That's why Mini Mike is hiding when Jesus turns around. Is Jesus angry? No, now He tells the woman that she is healed because she believes in Jesus. "I do, too," Mini Mike says to himself, but luckily he is not sick.

Questions

1. Where are the people standing on top of each other?
2. Can you see a boy giving money to a blind beggar?
3. Find the man doing handstands on a donkey.
4. Have you found the people standing sideways on a wall?
5. Do you see a computer?

Read

Mark 5:24-34

At once Jesus realized that power had gone out from Him. He turned around in the crowd and asked, "Who touched My clothes?"

"You see the people crowding against You," His disciples answered, "and yet You can ask, 'Who touched Me?'"

- Mark 5:30-31

Jesus Feeds the Five Thousand

Mike is thinking to himself, "Isn't this Jesus fantastic." He saw Him take the loaves and the fish into His hands and bless them. Mike was watching very carefully, but he still could not see how Jesus did it. Now all of a sudden, there is plenty of food, enough for all five thousand people.

Questions

1. Who has the most bread?
2. Two people – and a cat – have already eaten their fish, leaving only the bones, have you found them?
3. Which toys can you find?
4. Do you think people had balloons at that time?
5. Where is the photographer?
6. Where is Jesus?

Read

Mark 6:30-44

Taking the five loaves and the two fish and looking up to heaven, He gave thanks and broke the loaves. Then He gave them to His disciples to set before the people. He also divided the two fish among them all. They all ate and were satisfied, and the disciples picked up twelve basketfuls of broken pieces of bread and fish. The number of the men who had eaten was five thousand.

- Mark 6:41-44

Zaccheus the Tax Collector

Zaccheus is a rich chief tax collector, but he is a short man. Look up in the tree, there is Zaccheus. Can you see him? Mike has located him, but he can hardly see Jesus. He hears Him though. Jesus is calling, "Come down, Zaccheus, I want to visit you today." How excited Zaccheus is. Jesus is the one Person he really wants to have in his home.

Questions

1. Can you see a turtle?
2. Find the two dogs standing on their hind legs?
3. Almost everybody is looking for Jesus or on their way to see Him. Can you find any people who are busy with other things.
4. Where are the two people being carried on stretchers?

Read

Luke 19:1-10

When Jesus reached the spot, He looked up and said to him, "Zaccheus, come down immediately. I must stay at your house today."

- Luke 19:5

20

The Triumphal Entry

Mini Mike has never seen so many people so excited. Jesus is very popular as He rides into Jerusalem on a donkey. People think He is going to become a king and Mike can hear them calling, "King of Israel!" and "Hosanna!" Mike thinks it sounds great. You can see how the crowd is waving palm branches and many have thrown carpets onto the road.

Questions

1. Find the street cleaner leaning on his broom.
2. Where is the man in a wheelchair?
3. Can you see a child waving a noisemaker?
4. Have you found the man standing on one arm?
5. Look for the closed umbrella.

Read

John 12:12-19

The next day the great crowd that had come for the Feast heard that Jesus was on His way to Jerusalem. They took palm branches and went out to meet Him, shouting, "Hosanna!"

"Blessed is He who comes in the name of the Lord!"

"Blessed is the King of Israel!"

- John 12:12-13

The Holy Spirit Comes at Pentecost

Mike is astonished. This is the strangest thing he has ever seen. He knew all right that Pentecost was about the Holy Spirit. But he didn't know that the Spirit came like fire. Mike can hear the disciples suddenly speaking in different languages. He can even hear some (Danish) words. Mike says to Peter, "Do you think that I could receive the Holy Spirit, too?"

Questions

1. Find the artist painting.
2. Where are the two ladies who are being carried?
3. Can you see a turtle standing on its hind legs?
4. Point to the man riding an ostrich.
5. Have you found the small picture of Jesus on the cross?

Read

Acts 2:1-13

Suddenly a sound like the blowing of a violent wind came from heaven and filled the whole house where they were sitting. They saw what seemed to be tongues of fire that separated and came to rest on each of them. All of them were filled with the Holy Spirit and began to speak in other tongues as the Spirit enabled them.

- Acts 2:2-4

24

The Apostles Heal Many

It is obvious for Mike that the disciples have received the Holy Spirit. He watches how all the people around them are being healed. That is why more and more people keep coming. The disciples are saying that it is Jesus who heals through the Holy Spirit, even though Jesus is in heaven with God. Mike thinks to himself, "That's hard to understand," but he knows deep down it is true.

Questions

1. What is the man on the table doing?
2. Where is the man who is hard of hearing?
3. Find the five people walking in single file. Why are they doing that?
4. Can you see some people who have been healed?
5. Have you noticed a very clever cat?

Read

Acts 5:12-16

As a result, people brought the sick into the streets and laid them on beds and mats so that at least Peter's shadow might fall on some of them as he passed by. Crowds gathered also from the towns around Jerusalem bringing their sick and those tormented by evil spirits, and all of them were healed.

- Acts 5:15-16

Stephen

How wicked these people are. Stephen has just told them about Jesus, how He was killed on the cross, and now the people are stoning Stephen. Mini Mike has not told anyone that he believes in Jesus. Yet he is afraid that somebody might see him.

Questions

1. How many people are hunting Stephen down?
2. Which of them have rocks in their hands?
3. Who else besides Mini Mike do you think is on Stephen's side?
4. Find the nest with baby birds.
5. Where are the children?

Read

Acts 6:8-15 and 7:54-60

At this they covered their ears and, yelling at the top of their voices, they all rushed at him, dragged him out of the city and began to stone him.

- Acts 7:57-58

The Great Multitude in White Robes

What a party! This is the best party - and the biggest - Mike has ever been to. Together with these many, many people, Mike has received a white robe. It is the wedding of the Lamb. Mike knows that the Lamb is Jesus. Everybody is crying out in a loud voice, "Hallelujah! Our Lord God Almighty reigns!" Where is Mike? He is waving his hands and cheering just like the others.

Questions

1. Find the angel with no head.
2. Which countries or places in the world do you think these people come from?
3. Where is the man with a beard and glasses?
4. Can you see a man with his right hand over his heart?
5. Do you believe we shall be wearing glasses in Heaven?

Read

Revelation 19:6-9

Let us rejoice and be glad and give Him glory! For the wedding of the Lamb has come, and His bride has made herself ready.

- Revelation 19:7

Here are some of the things Mini Mike found on his journey through the New Testament. Unfortunately, he can't remember where he found them. Can you help him out?

Questions

Guess what this bottle contains. See if you can find it.

This bird is easy to recognize.

These two small people are far away. Do you think you can find them?

What do you think this is for?

This is a wastebasket. Can you find it?

Obviously, this foot is going somewhere. Do you know where it is?

Where did you see this flag?

Do you recognize this cat?

Where can you find this happy face?

This vase has been knocked down. What happened?

Doesn't that look like a bird? Where is it?

See if you can find this face.

This looks like it contains water. Where can you find it?

Doesn't this look like a piece of pottery? Can you find it?